AUG 1 3 2020

JB REEVES

A BEACON  BIOGRAPHY

KEANU REEVES

Michael DeMocker

PURPLE TOAD
PUBLISHING

PURPLE TOAD
PUBLISHING

Printing   1   2   3   4   5   6   7   8   9

A Beacon Biography

Library of Congress Cataloging-in-Publication Data
DeMocker, Michael
   Keanu Reeves / Written by: Michael DeMocker
      p.cm.
Includes bibliographic references, glossary, and index.
ISBN 978-1-62469-527-8
1. Reeves, Keanu, 1964– — Juvenile literature. 2. Motion picture actors — United States — Biographies — Juvenile literature. Series: I. A Beacon Biography.

PN2287.R295 D46 2020
791.43/028/092 B

Library of Congress Control Number: 2019948967

eBook ISBN: 9781624695261

ABOUT THE AUTHOR: Despite being a dashingly handsome, globetrotting, award-winning photojournalist and travel writer based in New Orleans, Michael DeMocker is, in truth, really quite dull, a terrible dancer, and a frequent source of embarrassment to his wife, son, and two dogs of varying intelligence. He once made a pilgrimage to the Circle K in Arizona where *Bill & Ted's Excellent Adventure* was filmed.

PUBLISHER'S NOTE: This story has not been authorized or endorsed by Keanu Reeves.

CONTENTS

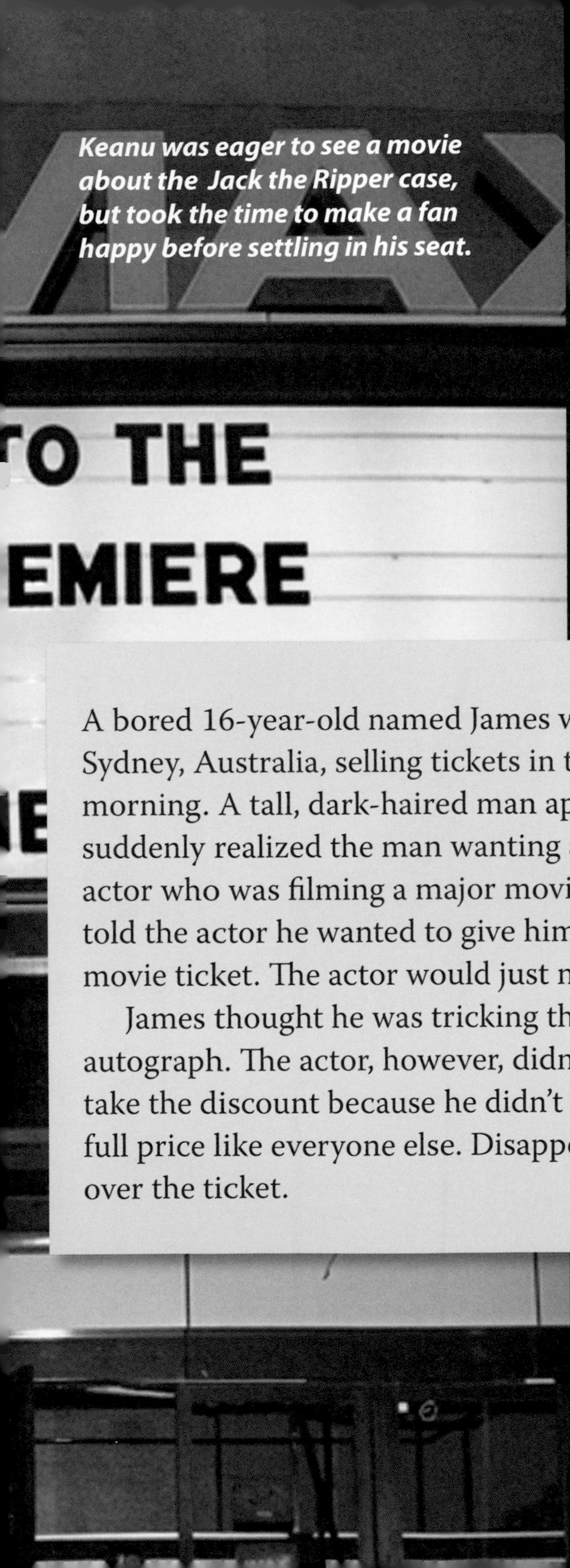

Keanu was eager to see a movie about the Jack the Ripper case, but took the time to make a fan happy before settling in his seat.

O THE

EMIERE

A Chance Meeting

A bored 16-year-old named James was working at a movie theater in Sydney, Australia, selling tickets in the box office on a slow weekday morning. A tall, dark-haired man approached the booth. James suddenly realized the man wanting a ticket was a famous Hollywood actor who was filming a major movie in the city. Thinking quickly, he told the actor he wanted to give him his employee discount for the movie ticket. The actor would just need to sign a logbook.

James thought he was tricking the actor into giving him an autograph. The actor, however, didn't think it was right for him to take the discount because he didn't work there. He insisted he pay full price like everyone else. Disappointed, the young man handed over the ticket.

Keanu had come to the theater to see Johnny Depp as famed inspector Frederick Abberline, the Scotland Yard detective who pursued Jack the Ripper in the 1880s.

A few minutes later, James heard a knock at the door to his ticket booth. It was the actor. "I realized you probably wanted my autograph," he said, "so I signed this."[1] The actor handed over a receipt from the theater's popcorn stand, with a signature that read "Keanu Reeves." Keanu [kee-AH-noo] figured out what James was trying to do and bought an ice cream cone just to get a receipt he could sign for James. He didn't even want the ice cream cone. He threw it away before going in to see the movie.

Eighteen years later, James became a writer. He wrote about the incident at the theater around the time Keanu's newest movie, *John Wick 3—Parabellum,* was released. It was just one of many stories that have emerged over the years of how the famous Hollywood actor does not behave like a privileged celebrity, but like an everyday, average guy. A big reason for Keanu's kind and easygoing personality can be found in his busy childhood.

Despite his fame, Keanu takes the time to pose with fans and to talk to them.

Keanu's childhood involved moves to several countries before the family finally found some stability in Canada.

A Vagabond Childhood

Keanu Charles Reeves was born on September 2, 1964, in Beirut, Lebanon. His father, Samuel Reeves, was a 19-year-old American geologist, a native of Hawaii whose mother was part Hawaiian and part Chinese. Keanu's name is Hawaiian for "cool breeze over the mountains." His mother, Patricia, was a 21-year-old showgirl and costume designer from Essex in England. She had been performing at a casino in Beirut when she met and married Samuel.

The family moved to Sydney, Australia, where Keanu's sister Kim was born. The marriage, however, did not last. Samuel abandoned the family when Keanu was just three years old. He went on to have a difficult life, ending up in a Hawaiian jail for selling drugs.

After his parents' divorce, Keanu's life lacked stability. Patricia moved Keanu and Kim to New York City and then to Toronto, Canada. She went through three more unsuccessful marriages, one to a stage and film director, another to a rock music promoter, and finally to a hair dresser. From his mother's various marriages, Keanu gained two stepsisters: Karina and Emma. Nannies and grandparents often cared for Keanu and his sisters.

Fun fact: Keanu is left-handed.

All the moving affected Keanu as an adult. Years later, he would say, "I've had a vagabond life. There is a bit of the gypsy in me, and living that way seemed to make sense. I couldn't settle down. I liked going to new places—renting apartments, staying in hotels."[1]

Despite the instability of his childhood, Keanu does credit his mother with bringing up her children properly. "Even for a runaway English girl, my mother gave us a proper upbringing. We learned manners, respect for our elders, formal table settings." He also learned how to be accepting of other people.[2]

In Toronto, Keanu attended five high schools in four years—and sometimes got into trouble. He wasn't the most interested student, but he did discover a passion for playing ice hockey. He became a star goalie who acquired the nickname "The Wall" because the puck couldn't get past him. A former teammate remembered, "I'd seen him play a handful of games at a competitive level, and despite him not having much formal training, he stood out. He was a raw talent, acrobatic and unrefined, but he could steal wins."[3] Keanu was even offered a professional tryout with the Windsor Spitfires of the Ontario Hockey League, but he turned down the chance. "I loved hockey, but I never wanted it to become too serious," he would remember years later.[4]

What he was becoming serious about was acting. It was in high school that Keanu discovered this passion. "We were reading *Romeo and Juliet* aloud in class and somehow through Shakespeare I found a way to express myself. It was a natural fit for me. . . . I went to my mother afterward and asked, 'Is it OK if I be an actor?' She said, 'Do whatever you like to do.' "[5]

Keanu began getting roles in made-for-TV movies and in plays in Canada. Despite choosing acting over hockey, it was hockey that helped him land his first role in a major movie. He played a French-Canadian hockey goalie in the 1986 sports film *Youngblood*, starring Rob Lowe and Patrick Swayze.

After that, Keanu dropped out of high school and headed to Los Angeles to continue his acting career.

In preparing for his role in the hockey movie Youngblood, *Keanu worked with former NHL player Eric Nesterenko (center), who had won the Stanley Cup with the 1961 Chicago Blackhawks.*

Keanu's career was about to explode, thanks to the acclaimed drama The River's Edge.

Chapter 3

Chuck Spadina Goes to L.A.

Upon arriving in Los Angeles, Keanu found he had trouble getting auditions because casting agents thought his name was too difficult to say. He started using stage names, like Chuck Spadina and Page Templeton III. In the end, though, he just used his real name at the auditions.

Keanu's big acting break came when he auditioned for the dark crime drama *The River's Edge.* This movie is about a group of teens dealing with a horrible crime committed by one of their friends. Casting director Carrie Frazier remembers seeing Keanu walk in for his audition. "He walked in the door, and I went, 'Oh my god, this is my guy!' It was just because of the way he held his body—his shoes were untied, and what he was wearing looked like a young person growing into being a man. I was over the moon about him."[1]

Over the next few years, Keanu went on to play the lead in a variety of movies, including the romantic comedy *The Night Before* (1988) and the dramatic comedy *The Prince of Pennsylvania* (1988).

He also got to work alongside acting legends in the movie *Dangerous Liaisons.* This period drama is set in eighteenth-century

Paris. Playing a French nobleman, Keanu worked with three A-list actors: Glenn Close, John Malkovich, and Michelle Pfeiffer.

The following year, Keanu was cast with Alex Winter in a film that would vault him to fame. It would also set the tone for his roles for years to come. He played Theodore "Ted" Logan in the hit *Bill & Ted's Excellent Adventure* (1989). Ted and Winter's character, Bill S. Preston, Esq., are a pair of dimwitted high school slackers who must pass a history class. If they don't, not only will the best friends be split up, but the future of humanity will be on the line. Luckily, they get help from a time-traveler, played by comedian George Carlin. He takes them back through time to collect historical figures, whom they present in person during their successful final history project. The movie was so unexpectedly popular, the pair made sequels called *Bill & Ted's Bogus Journey* (1991) and *Bill & Ted Face the Music* (2020).

Alex Winter costarred with Keanu in the hit movie **Bill & Ted's Excellent Adventure.**

Keanu's successful turn as Ted led him to be typecast in subsequent movies. This means he was hired, or cast, to play just one type of character. He played other dimwitted characters in *Parenthood* (1989) and *I Love You to Death* (1990).

In his next movie, Keanu broke out of this typecasting by appearing as an action hero. He played rookie FBI agent Johnny Utah who goes undercover to capture a gang of surfing bank robbers. Keanu again costarred with Patrick

Swayze in this film, called *Point Break* (1991).

Also in 1991, Keanu was shopping in a Los Angeles grocery store when he noticed a guy named Rob Mailhouse wearing a hockey jersey. Rob remembers the encounter: "This guy comes up to me and says, 'Hey, do you play hockey' and I said, 'yeah, I do actually' and he said, 'I'd like to play in a pick-up game.' "[2] The two hit it off and discovered they shared not just a love of hockey but of music. They started an alternative rock band called Dogstar. In the following years, the band met with some success, opening for rock legends like Bon Jovi and David Bowie. The band, however, was not destined for greatness and eventually broke up. As Keanu joked, "I guess it would have helped if our band was better."[3]

Keanu playing bass guitar with his band Dogstar in 1997

In 1991, his beloved sister Kim was diagnosed with leukemia at the age of 25. Keanu was very attentive to her as she battled the cancer. One of his friends remembers, "When she was in the hospital, he was there with her all the time, sitting at her bedside, holding her hand."[4] The leukemia finally went into remission, meaning there was no longer any sign of the disease in her body in 1999.

Because of his sister's battle with the disease, Keanu set up a private foundation to fund children's hospitals and to support cancer research. He chose not to put his famous name on it: "I don't like to attach my name to it, I just let the foundation do what it does", he says.[5]

Wynona Ryder and Keanu Reeves have been close friends for over 30 years, having made 4 films together during that time. She still jokingly refers to Reeves as her husband.

Chapter 4

Success and Tragedy

After his turn as an action star in *Point Break*, Keanu took on more challenging roles, such as that of drifter Scott Favor in *My Own Private Idaho* (1991). Written and directed by Gus Van Sant, the movie is a modern retelling of Shakespeare's plays *Henry IV, Parts One* and *Two*, and *Henry V*. The film costarred Keanu's friend River Phoenix, who received much critical praise for his acting in the film.

In 1992, Keanu starred with Gary Oldman and Winona Ryder in *Bram Stoker's Dracula*. In one scene, Keanu and Winona's characters get married. The director used a real Romanian priest, who performed a full ceremony. Years later, Winona contended she and Keanu may actually be married in real life because of the scene. Says Keanu, "Once in a while, I will get a text, 'Hello, husband . . .' I didn't really believe her, and then Francis Ford Coppola, the director of *Dracula*, contacted Winona and said publicly that, yeah, that really happened, the priest did a full ceremony, and Winona and I got married."[1]

Sadly, in 1993, Keanu's good friend and costar River Phoenix died of a drug overdose. Keanu finds it hard to talk about his friend's death. "I was terribly, terribly, terribly sad," he said. "Incredibly sad. And, um, I miss him very much."[2]

River Phoenix was an award-winning actor and a good friend of Keanu's. They starred together in the movie My Own Private Idaho. Sadly, the young actor died of a drug overdose outside a West Hollywood nightclub at the age of 23.

When River died, Keanu was filming *Speed*, a blockbuster that returned him to the action genre. Keanu plays a Los Angeles Police Department SWAT team member trying to save a busload of people from a mad bomber who has rigged the bus to explode if its speed drops below 50 miles per hour. The movie was a huge hit.

Keanu, however, refused to do the sequel called *Speed 2: Cruise Control* because he didn't like the script. As he recalls, "They said, 'You've got to do this' and I said, 'I read the script and I can't. It's called *Speed*, and it's on a cruise ship.'"[3] The movie, with another actor cast in the main role, was a huge flop.

Over the next few years, Keanu acted in a variety of independent dramas, romantic comedies, horror thrillers, and action films. For 1997's *The Devil's Advocate*, it was widely reported that Keanu took a big cut in his salary so that the producers could hire the legendary actor Al Pacino to costar with him. It was not the only time he would make this sacrifice. He made a similar deal so that the studio could afford to hire the famed actor Gene Hackman for the sports movie *The Replacements* (2000).

While *The Devil's Advocate* was well received, Keanu's other roles during this period of his career were not as memorable. Some people thought that his refusal to do *Speed 2* put him in "movie jail," where he was not being offered better roles.

But soon, he landed one of the biggest roles of his career.

In *The Matrix* (1999), Keanu plays Neo, a computer hacker. He must battle intelligent machines that trap people in an imitation reality. The action thriller features groundbreaking special effects. The film was a huge hit and spawned two sequels, *The Matrix Reloaded* and *The Matrix Revolutions* (both 2003). Keanu was so grateful to the special effects and costume teams that he gave up some of his share of the film's profits in order to help fund their departments. The move cost

Keanu's signature look in the Matrix trilogy had fans around the world copying his style.

The iconic coat worn by Keanu in The Matrix Reloaded is on display at the Science Fiction and Fantasy Hall of Fame in Seattle.

him millions of dollars, but, he said, "Money is the last thing I think about. I could live on what I have already made for the next few centuries."[4]

Between the first *Matrix* movie and its sequels, Keanu starred in the previously mentioned *The Replacements* (2000), a supernatural thriller called *The Gift* (2000), and the romantic comedy *Sweet November* (2001). Also in 2000, he played a serial killer in the *The Watcher*. However, he claims he was tricked into playing the role. "I never found the script interesting, but a friend of mine forged my signature on the agreement. I couldn't prove he did and I didn't want to get sued, so I had no other choice but to do the film."[5] The movie generally got negative reviews, with some reviewers saying Keanu was miscast as the creepy villain.

It was also in between the *Matrix* films that tragedy struck. Keanu had met a young actor named Jennifer Syme at a party in

1998, held in honor of his rock band Dogstar. They fell in love and in 1999 were expecting a daughter. Sadly, eight months into the pregnancy, the couple lost the baby. The pain of the loss caused the end of their romantic relationship, but the couple remained good friends. Then, eighteen months later, Jennifer was killed in a car accident. Keanu took the losses hard. "I miss being a part of their lives and them being part of mine. I wonder what the present would be like if they were here—what we might have done together. I miss all the great things that will never be."[6]

Despite tragedies in his life, Keanu has continued to persevere as an actor and a person.

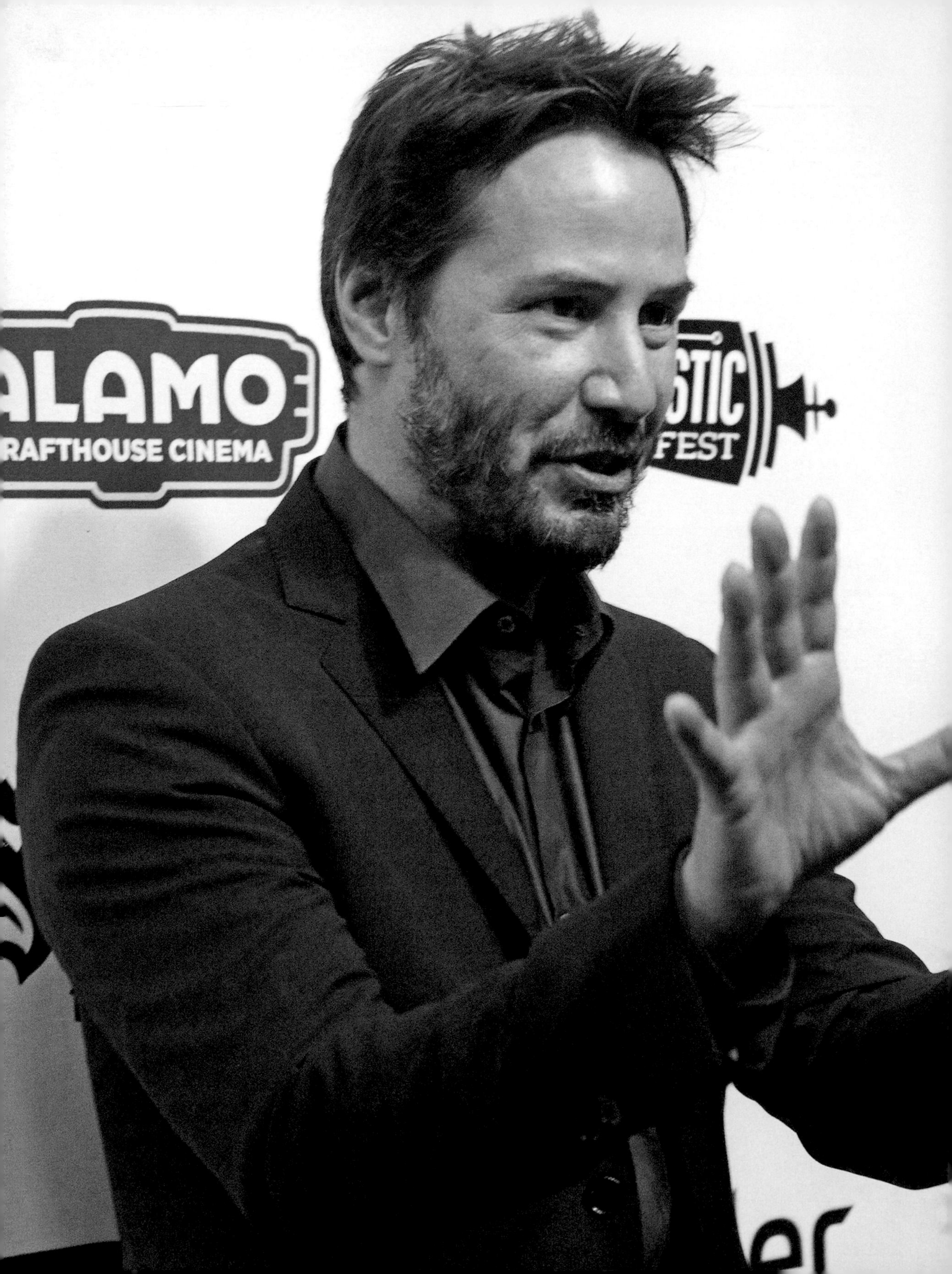
ALAMO
RAFTHOUSE CINEMA
STIC
FEST

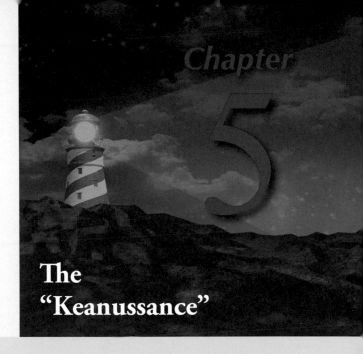

The "Keanussance"

Keanu speaks at the premiere of his wildly popular action movie *John Wick*, a film that marked the beginning of the resurgence of the long-time Hollywood icon.

After the Matrix trilogy was completed, Keanu spent the next ten years working on a variety of films. He even directed his first feature, the martial arts film *The Man of Tai Chi* (2013). However, none of them was as successful as his earlier films. He did receive a star on the Hollywood Walk of Fame in 2005.

Then, in 2014, he appeared in an action film called *John Wick*. The movie was an unexpected hit. Suddenly, Keanu was back at the top of Hollywood, not just because of the film's success, but also because of his generous personality.

Using tweets and cell phone videos, people began to share stories of Keanu acting like anything but a Hollywood star. A cell phone video from 2011 shows Keanu giving up his seat to a woman on the New York City subway. When it resurfaced a few years later, the clip went viral. People responded with other stories about the popular actor and how, unlike some celebrities, he was a genuinely nice person. One man remembered that as an eight-year-old boy, he saw Keanu at an airport just after *Bill & Ted's Excellent Adventure* came out. The boy worked up the courage to talk to the famous actor. Keanu sat and spoke to the young man and his older brother for 45 minutes.

In early 2019, Keanu was on a commercial flight from San Francisco to Los Angeles when the plane had to make an emergency landing in Bakersfield, California. Keanu helped organize several vans to drive the passengers the rest of the way home. Along the way, he read fun facts to his fellow passengers about the city of Bakersfield, saying, "Its population is around 380,000, making it the ninth most populous city in California and the 52nd most populous city in the nation."[1] He then played videos on his phone of music from Bakersfield musicians. Passengers posed for pictures with the down-to-earth celebrity, who took it all in stride.

Later that year, Keanu was filming the *Bill & Ted* sequel near New Orleans when he noticed a lawn sign put up by neighbors. It read, "You're Breathtaking," a reference to a line Keanu had spoken to a

Keanu doesn't travel with a huge entourage like some celebrities. He often rides the subway or takes commercial flights like the rest of us.

crowd at a videogame convention. He had said, "You're breathtaking! You're all breathtaking!"[2] Keanu stopped and knocked on the door of the house to talk with the fans, and then he asked if he could autograph the sign.

Another Internet user collected and posted a series of photos of Keanu posing with women, but respectfully keeping his hands off them during the photo. All the positive attention gave Keanu the nickname "The Internet's Boyfriend."

Fame even found Keanu accidentally in the world of online gaming. A character called the Reaper in the wildly

Keanu is happy to pose for photos with people when asked.

popular game Fortnight looks a lot like Keanu's bearded, suit-wearing character John Wick. The game's creative director said, "He was starting to have all these kids come up to him, all these teenagers on the street, and they weren't doing the normal, 'Oh you're Neo, oh you're Wick,'—they were doing, 'Fortnite guy! Fortnite guy!'"[3] With Keanu's blessing, the game designers went ahead and made an official John Wick character skin.

Comedians Keegan-Michael Key and Jordan Peele paid homage to Keanu by naming a comedy-action movie about a missing kitten after him.

In 2016, the comedy duo of Keegan-Michael Key and Jordan Peele made an action comedy about a pair of regular guys trying to rescue a cat from a gang of thugs. They named the cat and the movie *Keanu* after the actor. At first, the human Keanu did not have any interest in being a part of the movie. Then his sister, who had seen the first trailer for the movie, convinced him that the movie looked hilarious and he should join in. Keanu ended up happily voicing the cat in a dream sequence.

In 2019, the third *John Wick* movie was released, he voiced the Canadian daredevil Duke Caboom in *Toy Story 4*, and hundreds of stories of his kindness to strangers emerged. His career took off again in what journalists dubbed the Keaunussance [kee-AH-noo-zahntz]. The term

Keanu meets with the governor of São Paulo about filming a miniseries in Brazil's largest city.

is a play on the word Renaissance [REH-neh-zahntz], which means "rebirth."

Keanu even made fun of being a celebrity in the 2019 movie *Always Be My Maybe*. He plays a shallow, self-obsessed caricature of himself that is the opposite of his true personality.

By 2020, Keanu had appeared in over seventy films during his long and varied career. How long could the kind, talented Keanu, by this time in his mid-fifties, keep going? "As far as my legs can take me," he answers. "As far as the audience wants to go."[4]

With new **Matrix, John Wick,** *and* **Bill & Ted** *films on the horizon, Keanu doesn't look like he'll be slowing down any time soon.*

1964 Keanu Charles Reeves is born September 2 in Beirut, Lebanon.

1971 Keanu and his family move to Toronto, Canada.

1986 Keanu appears in the sports film *Youngblood* and the drama *The River's Edge*.

1988 He appears in *Dangerous Liaisons* with Glenn Close and John Malkovich.

1989 He has his first starring role as Ted in *Bill & Ted's Excellent Adventure*.

1991 He has his first action role in *Point Break*. With Rob Mailhouse, he forms the rock band Dogstar. His sister Kim is diagnosed with leukemia. He appears in the drama *My Own Private Idaho* with River Phoenix.

1993 His friend River Phoenix dies from a drug overdose.

1994 Keanu appears in the blockbuster movie *Speed*.

1999 He plays computer hacker Neo in the sci-fi thriller *The Matrix*. He and his girlfriend, Jennifer Syme, lose their daughter to miscarriage.

2001 Jennifer Syme dies in a car accident.

2005 Keanu receives a star on the Hollywood Walk of Fame.

2013 Keanu directs *The Man of Tai Chi*.

2016 The movie *Keanu* is released.

2019 Keanu appears in *Toy Story 4*, *John Wick 3*, and *Always Be My Maybe*.

2020 The third Bill & Ted movie, *Bill & Ted Face the Music*, is released.

SELECTED FILMOGRAPHY

2020 *Bill & Ted Face the Music*

2019 *Toy Story 4* (voice—animated movie)

2019 *Always Be My Maybe*

2019 *John Wick Chapter 3: Parabellum*

2017 *John Wick Chapter 2*

2016 *Keanu* (voice – movie)

2013 *The Man of Tai Chi* (director)

2014 *John Wick*

2005 *Constantine*

2003 *Matrix Revolutions*

2003 *Matrix Reloaded*

2000 *The Watcher*

2000 *The Replacements*

1999 *The Matrix*

1997 *The Devil's Advocate*

1995 *A Walk in the Clouds*

1994 *Speed*

1992 *Bram Stoker's Dracula*

1991 *My Own Private Idaho*

1991 *Point Break*

1989 *Bill & Ted's Excellent Adventure*

1988 *Dangerous Liaisons*

1986 *The River's Edge*

1986 *Youngblood*

Chapter 1

1. Estrella, Cicero. "Keanu Reeves Shows Sweet Disposition in Story Involving Ice Cream." *The Mercury News*, May 22, 2019. https://www.mercurynews.com/2019/05/21/keanu-reeves-shows-sweet-disposition-in-story-involving-ice-cream/

Chapter 2

1. Rader, Dotson. I Don't Want to Flee from Life. *Parade Magazine*, June 11, 2006.

2. Ibid.

3. Kay, Jason. "Keanu Reeves in the NHL? OK, Maybe a Stretch, but the Kid Had Mad Skills." *The Hockey News*, September 25, 2014. https://thehockeynews.com/news/article/keanu-reeves-in-the-nhl-ok-maybe-a-stretch-but-the-kid-had-mad-skills

4. Ibid.

5. Rader.

Chapter 3

1. Gilligan, Matt. "An Oral History of 'River's Edge,' 1987's Most Polarizing Teen Film." *Vice*, May 9, 2017. https://www.vice.com/en_us/article/bmwj3d/an-oral-history-of-rivers-edge-1987s-most-polarizing-teen-film

2. Fothergill, Lucas. "I Was in a Band with Keanu Reeves." *Vice*, July 14, 2015. www.vice.com/da/article/rbxq95/i-was-in-a-band-with-keanu-reeves

3. Pappademas, Alex. "The Legend of Keanu Reeves." *GQ*, April 15. 2019. https://www.gq.com/story/the-legend-of-keanu-reeves

4. Fowler, Bella. " 'Grief Never Ends.' Within Just 18 Months, Keanu Reeves Lost His Baby and the Love of His Life." *MSN*, March 245, 2019. www.msn.com/en-au/entertainment/other/grief-never-ends-within-just-18-months-keanu-reeves-lost-his-baby-and-the-love-of-his-life/ar-BBV9vry

5. O'Brien, Virginia. "Ways Keanu Has Secretly Given Away Millions." *The List*, n.d. www.thelist.com/93417/ways-keanu-secretly-given-away-millions

Chapter 4

1. Fernandez, Alexia. "Keanu Reeves Says Winona Ryder Calls Him 'Husband' after Revealing They Might Have Gotten Married for Real." *Entertainment Weekly*, January 8, 2019. https://ew.com/celebrity/2019/01/08/keanu-reeves-winona-ryder-husband/

2. Rochlin, Margy. "Keanu Reeves: The US Interview." *US Magazine*, March 1995.

3. Collin, Robbie. "Keanu Reeves: 'I Felt Like I Was Fighting for My Life.' " *The Telegraph*, April 9, 2015. www.telegraph.co.uk/film/john-wick/keanu-reeves-interview

4. O'Brien, Virginia. "Ways Keanu Has Secretly Given Away Millions." *The List*, n.d. www.thelist.com/93417/ways-keanu-secretly-given-away-millions.

5. "Keanu: I Was Tricked into Making Film." *The Guardian*, September 11, 2001. www.theguardian.com/film/2001/sep/11/news

6. Rader, Dotson." I Don't Want to Flee from Life." *Parade Magazine*, June 11, 2006.

Chapter 5

1. Price, Robert. "Keanu Reeves, Diverted to Bakersfield Airport, Makes the Best of It". *Bakersfield.com*, March 26, 2019. www.bakersfield.com/news/keanu-reeves-diverted-to-bakersfield-airport-makes-the-best-of/article_c5a92510-4fdf-11e9-9557-077592ee7952.html

2. Yam, Kimberly. "Just Keanu Reeves Telling a Crowd, 'You're All Breathtaking.' " *The Huffington Post*, June 10, 2019. www.huffpost.com/entry/keanu-reeves-breathtaking-e3_n_5cfe898fe4b0aab91c09b3d0

3. Cuthbertson, Anthony. "Keanu Reeves Called 'Fortnite Guy' So Much He Decided to Make Official John Wick Skin, Epic Games Reveals." *The Independent*, June 12 2019. www.independent.co.uk/life-style/gadgets-and-tech/gaming/keanu-reeves-fortnite-john-wick-skin-epic-games-a8954966.html

4. Pappademas, Alex. "The Legend of Keanu Reeves." *GQ*, April 15. 2019. https://www.gq.com/story/the-legend-of-keanu-reeves

Works Consulted

Botnar, Katy. "*A-List Actor Keanu Reeves: His Family and Tragically Heartbreaking Life.*" BodyHeightWeight.com, 16 April 2019. https://bodyheightweight.com/keanu-reeves-family/ Accessed July 2019.

Collin, Robbie. "Keanu Reeves: 'I Felt Like I Was Fighting for My Life.' " *The Telegraph*, April 9, 2015. www.telegraph.co.uk/film/john-wick/keanu-reeves-interview

Cuthbertson, Anthony. "Keanu Reeves Called 'Fortnite Guy' So Much He Decided to Make Official John Wick Skin, Epic Games Reveals." *The Independent*, June 12, 2019. www.independent.co.uk/life-style/gadgets-and-tech/gaming/keanu-reeves-fortnite-john-wick-skin-epic-games-a8954966.html

Estrella, Cicero. "Keanu Reeves Shows Sweet Disposition in Story Involving Ice Cream." *The Mercury News*, May 22, 2019. https://www.mercurynews.com/2019/05/21/keanu-reeves-shows-sweet-disposition-in-story-involving-ice-cream/

Fernandez, Alexia. "Keanu Reeves Says Winona Ryder Calls Him 'Husband' after Revealing They Might Have Gotten Married for Real." *Entertainment Weekly*, January 8, 2019. https://ew.com/celebrity/2019/01/08/keanu-reeves-winona-ryder-husband/

Fothergill, Lucas. "I Was in a Band with Keanu Reeves." *Vice*, July 14, 2015. www.vice.com/da/article/rbxq95/i-was-in-a-band-with-keanu-reeves

Fowler, Bella. " 'Grief Never Ends.' Within Just 18 Months, Keanu Reeves Lost His Baby and the Love of His Life." *MSN*, March 245, 2019. www.msn.com/en-au/entertainment/other/grief-never-ends-within-just-18-months-keanu-reeves-lost-his-baby-and-the-love-of-his-life/ar-BBV9vry

Fry, Naomi. "Keanu Reeves Is Too Good for This World." *The New Yorker*, June 3, 2019. www.newyorker.com/culture/culture-desk/keanu-reeves-is-too-good-for-this-world

Gilligan, Matt. "An Oral History of 'River's Edge,' 1987's Most Polarizing Teen Film." *Vice*, May 9, 2017. https://www.vice.com/en_us/article/bmwj3d/an-oral-history-of-rivers-edge-1987s-most-polarizing-teen-film

Kaufman, Amy. "How Key and Peele Got Keanu Reeves to Voice a Cat in 'Keanu.' " *Los Angeles Times*, April 25, 2016. www.latimes.com/entertainment/movies/moviesnow/la-et-mn-keanu-reeves-cat-key-peele-20160425-story.html

Kay, Jason. "Keanu Reeves in the NHL? OK, Maybe a Stretch, but the Kid Had Mad Skills." *The Hockey News*, September 25, 2014. https://thehockeynews.com/news/article/keanu-reeves-in-the-nhl-ok-maybe-a-stretch-but-the-kid-had-mad-skills

"Keanu: I Was Tricked into Making Film." *The Guardian*, September 11, 2001. www.theguardian.com/film/2001/sep/11/news

Lang, Cady. "Keanu Reeves Was the Best Companion on a Bus Ride with a Bunch of Stranded Plane Passengers." *Time*, March 25, 2019. https://time.com/5558494/keanu-reeves-bus/

Le Vine, Lauren. "Keanu Reeves Has Some Thoughts About The "Keanussance". Refinery29.com, June 13, 2019. https://www.refinery29.com/en-us/2019/06/235279/keanu-reeves-keanussance-toy-story-4-john-wick-always-be-my-maybe Accessed July 2019 Accessed July 2019.

Maslin, Janet. "Review/Film; Surf's Up For F.B.I. in Bigelow's 'Point Break.'" *The New York Times*, July 12, 1991. www.nytimes.com/1991/07/12/movies/review-film-surf-s-up-for-fbi-in-bigelow-s-point-break.html

Moran, Lee. "Story About Keanu Reeves Buying Ice Cream Goes Viral for the Sweetest Reason." *The Huffington Post*, May 21, 2019. www.huffpost.com/entry/keanu-reeves-ice-cream-story_n_5ce3d6e9e4b0e69c18f17ec9

O'Brien, Virginia. "Ways Keanu Has Secretly Given Away Millions." *The List*, n.d. www.thelist.com/93417/ways-keanu-secretly-given-away-millions

Pappademas, Alex. "The Legend of Keanu Reeves." *GQ*, April 15, 2019. https://www.gq.com/story/the-legend-of-keanu-reeves

Price, Robert. "Keanu Reeves, Diverted to Bakersfield Airport, Makes the Best of It". *Bakersfield.com* March 26, 2019. www.bakersfield.com/news/keanu-reeves-diverted-to-bakersfield-airport-makes-the-best-of/article_c5a92510-4fdf-11e9-9557-077592ee7952.html

Rader, Dotson. "I Don't Want to Flee from Life." *Parade Magazine*, June 11, 2006.

Rochlin, Margy. "Keanu Reeves: The US Interview." *US Magazine*, March 1995.

Yam, Kimberly. "Just Keanu Reeves Telling a Crowd, 'You're All Breathtaking.' " *The Huffington Post*, June 10, 2019. www.huffpost.com/entry/keanu-reeves-breathtaking-e3_n_5cfe898fe4b0aab91c09b3d0

GLOSSARY

acrobatic (ak-roh-BAT-ik)—Skilled at jumping and moving the body with ease.

audition (aw-DIH-shun)—An interview and tryout for a singer or actor.

caricature (KAYR-ih-kah-chur)—A drawing or description of a person or thing that seems silly because it exaggerates something about it in a funny way.

celebrity (seh-LEB-rih-tee)—A famous person; a star.

director (dih–REK–tor)—In movies and television, the person who is in charge of the camera crews, actors, and all aspects of production of the final project.

geologist (jee-AH-luh-jist)—A scientist who studies rocks to understand the history of the planet.

leukemia (loo-KEE-mee-uh)—A type of cancer that affects the organs that make blood.

miscarriage (MIS-kayr-idj)—The loss of a baby before it is born.

passion (PASH-un)—A strong liking or love.

period drama (PEER-ee-id DRAH-mah)—A story that takes place during a particular time in history.

romantic comedy (roh-MAN-tik KAH-muh-dee)—A lighthearted story about finding true love.

special effects (SPEH-shul ee-FEKTS)—Images or sounds that are added to a movie to make it seem more real.

stage name—A fake name used by performers.

trilogy (TRIH-loh-jee)—A series of three related stories.

typecast (TYP-kast)—To be considered for only one type of role.

vagabond (VAG-uh-bond)—A person with no permanent home who wanders from place to place.

viral (VY-rul)—Quickly spread, such as by social media.